BIBLE VERSES TO REMEMBER SERIES

OUR
GREAT GOD

SALLY MICHAEL

Illustrated by
SENGSAVANE CHOUNRAMANY

Dedicated to Joyce Heinrich who has taught
many little children that God is great.
May you continue to exalt Christ to the next
generation until your last breath.

New Growth Press, Greensboro, NC 27401
Text Copyright © 2023 by Sally Michael
Illustration Copyright © 2023 by Sengsavane Chounramany

Cover/Interior Design and Typesetting: Dan Stelzer
Cover/Interior illustrations: Sengsavane Chounramany

ISBN: 978-1-64507-377-2
Library of Congress Control Number: 2023934674

Printed in India

30 29 28 27 26 25 24 23   1 2 3 4 5

FOR THE Lord IS A GREAT GOD, AND A GREAT KING ABOVE ALL GODS.

PSALM 95:3

What makes you so
happy you feel like singing?
How about puppy dogs and
bubbles? Butterflies and swings?

There are so many things to
sing about. Singing shows how
we feel and what is in our hearts.

The greatest of all reasons to sing is when we think about God.
All that we know and love about God should make us want to sing about him.

For the LORD is a great God,
and a great King above all gods.

Psalm 95:3

God is a great God! God made the sun to shine in the day
and the moon and stars to shine at night.

He made high mountains and deep oceans with waves that roll in and out, over and over, without stopping. He made quiet lakes and bubbling rivers, tall trees and sweet-smelling flowers.

God made all the animals, from the biggest to the smallest! And he made every boy and girl.

God made everything in the whole world!
For the LORD is a great God!

God is good and does good things. He feeds the birds, tells the sun to rise each day, and gives us air to breathe. God never sleeps and never gets tired. He is everywhere all the time.

God is always watching over his world, taking care of it.

God's love is never-ending. It never stops! God understands when we are weak, scared, or sad.

He is kind and generous.
He gives us all that we need and more!
God is also very wise.
He put seeds in flowers and trees
to give us more flowers and trees!

Do you know if it will rain tomorrow?
Do you know how many stars there are?

God knows everything!

He knows when it will rain.
He knows all the stars by name.
He knows every single thing
that happens. He knows every
secret and every whispered word.

He knows why he made elephants with long
trunks and pigs with short snouts. He knows
who you are and what you ate for breakfast!
For the Lord is a great God!

But there is even more to know about God!

He is a great King—greater than all kings!
God rules over the whole world and everyone in it!
His laws are for everyone, everywhere.

Our great God and King, who rules over all things,
knows every single person.

He knows your first and last name—even your middle name if you have one!

He knows exactly how many hairs are on your head.
If you pull out a hair, God knows how many hairs you have left!

He watches over you every minute of every day.
What great love he has for us!

How do you feel when you think about how great God is?

Are you amazed at his great power?

Is there anything he can't do?

No! He can do all things!

Think about all
the things that
God knows.

Try to imagine what it must
be like to know everything
about everything—to even
know things that haven't
happened yet! How should we
think and feel about the Lord,
the great God and King?

God cares for all the people in the world.
All that we know about God should make our hearts say,
"I love you, Almighty God! You are amazing, God!
You are a great God!"

This is called worship.

Worship is loving God and seeing his greatness.
It is knowing that he is the best of all.
Nothing is more important than God,
and no one is greater than God!

When we see God's greatness, it should make us want to sing!

We can clap and shout for joy to show that
we are so happy about how wonderful he is!

Sing to the Lord, the great God and King!

For the LORD is a great God,
and a great King above all gods.

Psalm 95:3

Children learn about God in baby steps—little steps of learning who he is, what he has done, and what he is doing now, plus little steps of obedience to his teaching and his ways. And, by God's grace, what they learn in little steps of trusting Jesus eventually grows into big steps of faith.

But children don't learn these things by themselves through their natural instincts. They learn them when they are taught the truths of God's Word. In Psalm 86:11, David humbly prays, "Teach me your way, O Lord." The ways of God are contrary to our sinful nature, which is why we must be taught by God (see also Proverbs 14:12 and Isaiah 55:8).

Teaching God's truth is necessary to lead children to obey the Lord from the heart. Children may obey God's commands simply because they like to please their parents or because it's expected of them. This can be a positive step, but it falls short of the kind of obedience that flows from personal conviction and love for God. Such conviction can only be brought about by teaching.

To come to saving faith, a child must embrace the whole of David's prayer in Psalm 86:11: "Teach me your way, O Lord, that I may walk in your truth; unite my heart to fear your name." Notice how he prays that the truth of God would affect his whole heart and life. Real, saving faith requires a change of heart. It requires embracing who God is and entrusting oneself completely to Jesus Christ.

God's Word can make your child "wise for salvation through faith in Christ Jesus" (2 Timothy 3:15). As you use God-breathed Scripture to teach, reprove, correct, and train your child in righteousness (2 Timothy 3:16), the Holy Spirit may chip away at your child's "heart of stone" and turn it into a "heart of flesh" (Ezekiel 36:26). Steps taken when little may lead your child to saving faith—to trusting in Jesus for the forgiveness of sin and the fulfillment of all his promises.

Your part as parent, grandparent, or other discipler of the next generation is to be a teacher, an example of walking in God's ways, and a model of a heart dedicated to God. May your prayer for yourself and your children each day be:

Teach me your way, O Lord,
that I may walk in your truth;
unite my heart to fear your name.
—Psalm 86:11

How to Use This Book

This book will encourage your child to trust Jesus and walk in his ways.
The goal is to instruct their mind, engage their heart, and influence their will.

To Instruct the Mind
- Read the book several times.
- Explain any words or concepts unfamiliar to your child.
- Help your child to memorize the verse.

To Engage the Heart
- Interact with your child as you read the book. Dialogue about God and his ways. Help your child to see God's greatness and goodness. (See *Helping Children to Understand the Gospel* in the resource list.)
- Encourage your child to trust God in everyday events.
- Pray that your child would be receptive to the truth, trust Christ, and walk in his ways.
- Pray with your child that Jesus would give them a heart to love and glorify God.

To Influence the Will
- Talk with your child about ways to apply the verse in real-life situations.
- Encourage your child to act on what they have learned and to practice obedience to the truth.
- Guide your child in walking in the truth and living what they have learned.

Other Resources for Parents:

The Disciple-Making Parent: A Comprehensive Guidebook for Raising Your Children to Love and Follow Jesus by Chap Bettis

Gospel-Powered Parenting: How the Gospel Shapes and Transforms Parenting by William P. Farley

Helping Children to Understand the Gospel by Sally Michael, Jill Nelson, and Bud Burk

Instructing a Child's Heart by Tedd and Margy Tripp

Mothers, Disciplers of the Next Generation by Sally Michael

Teach Them Diligently: How to Use the Scriptures in Child Training by Lou Priolo

Tips for Helping Young Children Memorize Scripture

Memorizing by repetition works well when teaching verses to young children:

1. **Say the reference.** First, clearly pronounce the reference. Then ask the child to repeat the reference. (You may want to explain that a reference is like an address that tells where to find a verse in the Bible.)

2. **Repeat the verse in sections.** Say the passage in several bite-sized sections, repeating each section with the child.

   For example:
   a. Parent: *In the beginning*; Parent and child: *In the beginning*
   b. Parent: *God created*; Parent and child: *God created*
   c. Parent: *the heavens and the earth*; Parent and child: *the heavens and the earth*

3. **Repeat the reference.**

4. **Review the verse** several more times lengthening the sections each time, giving the reference before and after the passage.

5. **Discuss the verse.** After the passage is memorized (usually in 3-4 repetitions), it is good to dissect it. Explain the meaning of unfamiliar words. Rephrase the passage and talk about how the verse applies to life.

Memory Verse Resources:

"Foundation Verse Cards." Verse cards for 2- to 5-year-olds in ESV or NIV. Truth78. https://www.truth78.org/foundation-verses-resources.

"Foundation Verse Coloring Book." Truth78.org

Fighter Verses. App for Apple or Android (includes Foundation Verses)

LIVING BY THE WORD

What can you do to help remember to give God glory for all the things that he has done?

Sing worship songs as a family. You could sing along with recorded songs. Wave ribbons or scarves and clap your hands!

Make a crown and decorate it with pretty colors, stamps, markers, stickers, shiny paper, plastic jewels, etc. Make the crown very special to show how special God is. Write the words: "God is a great King!" on the crown.

Memorize Psalm 95:3. "For the LORD is a great God, and a great King above all gods."

Pray this prayer every day: *"Teach me your way, O LORD, that I may walk in your truth; unite my heart to fear your name" (Psalm 86:11).* Pray that you will learn what the Bible says about God and his ways, that you will obey God's Word, and that God will give you a new heart.